Teens and Marijuana

Other titles in the *Teen Choices* series include:

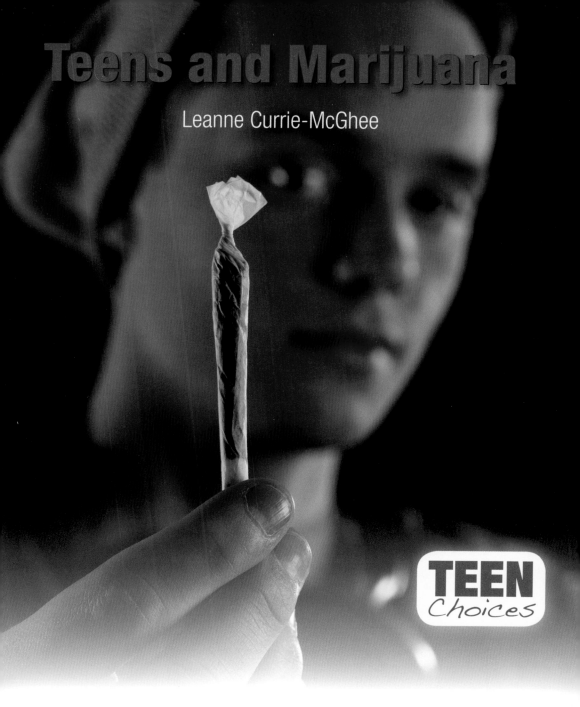

Teens and Marijuana

Leanne Currie-McGhee

TEEN *Choices*

ReferencePoint Press®

San Diego, CA

For more information, contact:
ReferencePoint Press, Inc.
PO Box 27779
San Diego, CA 92198
www.ReferencePointPress.com

LIBRARY OF CONGRESS CATALOGING-IN-PUBLICATION DATA

Currie-McGhee, Leanne.
  Teens and marijuana / by Leanne Currie-McGhee.
    pages cm. -- (Teen choices series)
  ISBN-13: 978-1-60152-914-5 (hardback)
  ISBN-10: 1-60152-914-7 (hardback)
  1. Teenagers--Drug use--United States. 2. Marijuana. I. Title.
  HV5824.Y68C872 2016
  362.29'50835--dc23
                                                        2014049497

Contents

A Teen Trend

In 2013 twenty-year-old Miley Cyrus decided to publicly share her love of marijuana. She stepped onto the stage at the MTV Europe Awards to accept an award for best song, "Wrecking Ball," as thousands of fans cheered. While everyone watched and TV cameras filmed, Cyrus joked, "I couldn't fit this award in my bag, but I did find this."[1] She then pulled a lighter and marijuana joint out of her Chanel handbag. Next she lit up and smoked for all to see. The footage of her actions was widespread and seen on the Internet by many of her fans. Around the world, teens watched as Cyrus proudly and blatantly smoked marijuana.

Cyrus does not see her marijuana use as a big deal or something to hide. "I was just walking out of my room and then I was like 'Oh I have [this joint] in my bag, that will be really funny,"[2] said Cyrus of her decision to smoke marijuana onstage. Cyrus is not the only celebrity who publicly touts marijuana use. Others, including Lady Gaga and Rihanna, often talk about marijuana as a harmless way to relax and have fun.

The fact that celebrities openly use marijuana does not, in all likelihood, alone convince teens to use marijuana. However, it does make the choice to experiment easier for teens who might wonder how smoking marijuana can be considered harmful when people who have achieved so much do it so openly. "Seeing these big celebs smoke proves that you can still be ambitious and accomplish a lot [while using marijuana],"[3] said Sarah, age nineteen.

Harmless Drug?

Supporting the belief that marijuana is harmless is the changing legal status of the drug. Marijuana used to be considered an illegal substance in all US states. However, in the past two decades, twenty-three states have legalized the use of marijuana for medical purposes if a doctor prescribes it. Four states have also legalized the recreational use of marijuana for those twenty-one and older.

On stage at the 2013 MTV Europe Awards, pop singer Miley Cyrus lit up and smoked a marijuana cigarette. Critics claim that such celebrity behavior can lead young people to question whether marijuana is truly harmful and whether marijuana laws are too restrictive.

Although marijuana use by teens is still illegal in all states except in special medical cases, the growing trend of legalization adds to the teen perception that marijuana use is not risky. "People use it as actual medicine, and it's not as poisonous as alcohol," said Sarah. "I never get a brutal hangover when I'm high, and it doesn't make me lose control like drinking does."[4] Sarah, like many other teens, does not consider the physical, social, and emotional dangers that marijuana can pose to teens.

Growing Popularity

The idea that marijuana is a "safe" drug has led to an increased percentage of teens who have tried marijuana and who have used it on a regular basis. The American Academy of Child and Adolescent Psychiatry states that in the past few years, marijuana use among teens has been at its highest level in thirty years. Rising levels of teen marijuana use can be seen in the results of various surveys, including the 2013 Youth Risk Behavior Surveillance System by the Centers for Disease Control and Prevention (CDC). When that survey was done in 1991, it found that 14.1 percent of high school students had used marijuana in the past thirty days. The same survey done in 2013 found that 23.4 percent of high school students had used marijuana in the past thirty days. According to this and other surveys, marijuana has become even more popular than smoking cigarettes among teens.

As with other drugs, peer pressure has been a driving factor in marijuana's popularity among teens. Teens will attempt to convince their friends to partake by telling them not only that it is fun, but also that it is not dangerous. Even those teens who understand there are dangers associated with marijuana can still be influenced to experiment. "At first I was scared to do it, knowing how bad it was," teenager Lily stated in Waterloo, Iowa's West High School student newspaper, "but I was stressed out, young and my friend kept telling me that nothing bad would happen, so I did."[5] Once Lily tried it, she continued to use and found herself changing. Her grades went down, she angered more easily, and she found herself turning to marijuana anytime she felt stressed out.

Deadly Results

Like Lily, teens who do become regular users of marijuana often discover that marijuana use is not always risk free. And in some instances it can be downright dangerous. Fatalities linked to marijuana use are not common but do occur. Levy Thamba was one of those unfortunate people whose experience with marijuana ended in tragedy.

Thamba, nineteen, was a student at Northwest College in Wyoming in 2014. One weekend he visited friends in Colorado, where recreational and medical marijuana are legal. One of the friends was twenty-three years old and therefore could legally buy marijuana edibles at a store. The store employee told the buyer to cut the marijuana-laced cookie into six pieces and only eat one piece at a time. Instead, the young man bought four cookies, one for himself and one each for three of his friends. Thamba took an entire Sweet Grass Kitchen lemon poppy seed cookie back to the hotel where he and his friends were staying. Thamba ate a piece and did not feel anything immediately, so he ate the entire cookie.

Thamba fell asleep but then woke several times and spoke incoherently. He went back to sleep again, but then, according to his friends, woke up and began smashing the room's furniture, lamps, and television. He ran outside the room and then tumbled over a railing that overlooked the hotel lobby. Thamba died from the fall. The local coroner listed "marijuana intoxication" as the cause of death. Thamba's case, while not usual, is an example of a real danger associated with marijuana.

"People use it as actual medicine, and it's not as poisonous as alcohol. I never get a brutal hangover when I'm high, and it doesn't make me lose control like drinking does."[4]

—Sarah, a nineteen-year-old who uses marijuana.

Education Is Key

To combat the dangers of teen marijuana use, many states are developing their own programs to educate teens. Unlike prevention efforts of an earlier generation that relied on scare tactics, these new programs focus mainly on teaching teens the benefits of delaying use of marijuana. These programs encourage them to make their own decisions without being influenced by other kids. The hope is that these programs will lead teens to make an independent decision to delay, as long as possible, using marijuana.

Most of these programs have been developed in states where medical marijuana—and in a few instances recreational marijuana—is now legal. These states want teens to understand that there are legitimate reasons why it is still *illegal* for teens to use marijuana. Health professionals believe that campaigns need to appeal to teens' common sense about what they want in life.

> **"This generation of kids wants good brains; they want to get into better schools. Talk to a junior or senior about whether marijuana use shaves a couple points off their SATs, and they will listen to you."**[6]
>
> —*Steve Pasierb, chief executive of the Partnership for Drug-Free Kids.*

"This generation of kids wants good brains; they want to get into better schools," says Steve Pasierb, the chief executive of the Partnership for Drug-Free Kids. "Talk to a junior or senior about whether marijuana use shaves a couple points off their SATs, and they will listen to you."[6] Pasierb believes that if teens know the risks of use, many will choose to abstain.

How successful such prevention efforts will be is unknown. What is understood by most people, however, is that marijuana is being used more commonly among teens and is more easily accessible than in decades past. If teens want to use marijuana, it is relatively easy to do so. What health professionals hope teens consider is that there are known dangers to teen use of marijuana; there are also many unknowns in connection with long-term use. Health professionals and others want teens to understand that their decisions regarding marijuana can have a serious impact on their future.

Chapter One

Teen Usage

Marijuana is currently the most popular illicit drug used by teenagers. For years marijuana use among teens had been declining. But in the first decade of the twenty-first century, this trend changed. As marijuana became more accepted for medical use, and even recreational use among adults, teens began to perceive marijuana as a harmless, enjoyable drug. Also, many teens found that marijuana was easy to obtain. Over the past decade, statistics show, a decreasing percentage of teens viewed marijuana as a drug that poses risks. The result is an increased percentage of teens experimenting with marijuana.

Paul began experimenting with marijuana at age fourteen. "I started using on a lark, a dare from a best friend who said that I was too chicken to smoke a joint and drink a quart of beer," he said. "I was fourteen at that time."[7] Soon Paul began using marijuana regularly and found that he was unable to stop. He developed negative feelings about himself and his abilities; he also became paranoid and no longer trusted his friends. Paul attributed all of these changes to his marijuana use. After seven years of heavy use, he decided to stop, but to do so, Paul needed the help of an addiction treatment program.

If fourteen sounds young to begin experimenting with marijuana, it is. But it is not uncommon; studies have shown that marijuana use among even younger teens is not unusual. The 2013 Monitoring the Future report, part of an annual study funded by the National Institute on Drug Abuse (NIDA), found that one out of six of eighth graders had tried marijuana. "We should be extremely concerned that 12 percent of 13- to 14-year-olds are using marijuana," commented physician and NIDA director

Nora D. Volkow. "The children whose experimentation leads to regular use are setting themselves up for declines in IQ and diminished ability for success in life."[8]

Marijuana use by both younger and older teens began to increase in the first decade of the 2000s and has continued to rise since then. From just 2012 to 2013, according to the Monitoring the Future study, the percentage of students who had used marijuana once or more in the previous twelve months rose from 11.4 percent to 12.7 percent among eighth graders and 28.0 percent to 29.8 percent among tenth graders; among twelfth graders, use held steady at 36.4 percent. Additionally, the study found that by the time teens graduated from high school, approximately 44 percent of students had tried marijuana at least once.

> "We should be extremely concerned that 12 percent of 13- to 14-year-olds are using marijuana."[8]
>
> —NIDA Director Nora D. Volkow.

Marijuana's Popularity

Marijuana is a mixture of the dried and shredded leaves, stems, seeds, and flowers of *Cannabis sativa*, the hemp plant. This plant originated in Asia and now is grown all over the world. It is an annual plant that can grow to a height of 8 to 12 feet (2.4 m to 3.7 m). People grow it both indoors and outdoors. Some grow the plant in large quantities, with the goal of selling and distributing it, and others grow it for their own personal use.

The psychoactive properties of marijuana are directly tied to the chemical tetrahydrocannabinol, or THC, that is found in the plant. This chemical is responsible for the "high" people feel when using marijuana. When marijuana is smoked, the THC quickly passes from the lungs into the bloodstream, which carries the chemical to the brain and other organs throughout the body. When it is eaten (or ingested), the same process takes place but at a slower pace, because the THC has to go through the gastrointestinal tract before entering the bloodstream.

Marijuana is derived from the dried leaves, stems, flowers, and seeds of the hemp plant. Hemp is grown around the world, and its fibers, seeds, and oils are used in making rope, cloth, paper, resins, fuels, and other products.

THC stimulates brain cells to release dopamine, which creates a euphoric feeling. This is the feeling that people are looking for when taking the drug. However, it also interferes with the hippocampus, which is the part of the brain that is involved in forming, organizing, and storing memories and also in connecting emotions and senses to memories. Because it affects the hippocampus, marijuana disrupts how information is processed, so it can result in hallucinations, changes in people's thinking, and delusions. Typically, the effects begin just a few minutes after smoking marijuana, and fifteen to thirty minutes after ingesting it, and then last about two hours.

Teens who experiment with marijuana often continue to use it in hopes of achieving the same feeling they got from their first experience. According to Andrew, a former teen user, "The first time you use, you're going to be way up here. The second time, you're going to be chasing that high feeling. The only reason you keep using is because you want to get up to that place."[9]

Increasing THC

The amount of THC in marijuana determines the strength of its effects. The buds, which are most often used in making the drug, contain 3 percent to 22 percent THC. People also use the hash oil, a honey-like resin from the plant, to make a stronger drug that is called hash. The resin contains three to five times more THC than the plant itself.

Over the past three decades, the THC in any form of marijuana has greatly increased due to growers' new methods for raising marijuana crops. In 2012 THC concentrations in marijuana averaged close to 15 percent, compared to around 4 percent in the 1980s. "You really have to be careful," stated Mahmoud ElSohly, director of the Marijuana Potency Project. "The danger of this high-potency material is not with the experienced marijuana smokers, but young people who really don't know what they're smoking. They don't know what to expect, and before they know it, they've inhaled too much."[10]

How Marijuana Is Used

There are several different ways that people take marijuana, ranging from smoking the leaves as joints to ingesting the leaves by cooking them in items like brownies. The most popular method is smoking a joint. A joint is a hand-rolled cigarette in which the marijuana leaves are rolled up into paper, and then the joint is smoked like a cigarette. Similar to this is a cigar, or blunt, which is smoked after filling a hollowed-out cigar with dried marijuana leaves. As social media has become more popular, teens have easily discovered how to make joints and blunts because people post this information. Obtaining the marijuana and putting the joints or blunts together is a relatively easy process, which is another reason marijuana is popular among teens.

Another way to use marijuana is to smoke it through a bong, or water pipe. Bongs are different than joints in that a bong cools the smoke before it enters a person's lungs, and a larger amount of smoke is inhaled at once. A bong works by filling the base with water, packing marijuana into a bowl that is attached, and igniting the marijuana. Then the user puts his or her lips on the bong's mouthpiece and inhales. The smoke rises through the water before entering the user's mouth, and the water acts as a coolant and a filter, taking out undesirable particles.

Some teens find bongs appealing because they can make them by themselves. Also, they have seen celebrities use bongs for marijuana. In 2014 singer Miley Cyrus posted pictures of herself on Instagram creating a bong. The twenty-one-year-old shared a photo and video of a homemade bong she crafted from fans' gifts. Cyrus created the bong using beads, ribbons, fake flowers, and rainbow bracelets. She released a picture of the final project, which was 5 feet (1.5 m) high and included multiple dinosaur toys, two strobe lights, and fake leaves.

Marijuana can also be ingested, which is often done through edibles, food products made with either the marijuana leaves or hash resin. Typically, the edibles are baked goods such as brownies and cookies, but lollipops and gummy candies have also

School Snacks

Bringing marijuana edibles to school might *sound* like fun but it does not always turn out that way. In December 2014 a seventeen-year-old Maryland high school student admitted to giving his teacher a brownie laced with marijuana. The student later told authorities that he gave the teacher the brownie when she asked him to share. The teacher had no idea that it contained marijuana; she ended up in the hospital. The student was charged with possession and distribution of a controlled substance, second-degree assault, and reckless endangerment.

become popular in medical and recreational marijuana stores. In the state of Washington, where marijuana is legal for both medical and recreational use, thirty-five different marijuana-infused foods and beverages have been approved by the Washington State Liquor Control Board. Foods include trail mix, chocolate bars, and peanut brittle. Beverages include coffee and soda that are infused with a liquid marijuana extract.

Many medical professionals worry about the growing popularity of edibles because often teens do not realize how potent they are. "With edibles, children and teens may consume higher quantities than the inhaled form. It takes much longer for the THC to go through the gut than to be inhaled, so a teen may not experience a 'high', which leads to eating more and more,"[11] said Dr. Yolanda Evans, an adolescent expert at Seattle Children's Hospital. The result is that teens may take quite a lot more than a normal amount and end up in the hospital.

> "With edibles, children and teens may consume higher quantities than the inhaled form."[11]
>
> —Dr. Yolanda Evans, adolescent expert at Seattle Children's Hospital.

Newer Usage

Using electronic cigarettes with marijuana is a newer method that teens have discovered. This method is becoming more popular because it is a way to mask marijuana use. Teens take the nicotine out of electronic cigarettes, called e-cigarettes, and replace it with marijuana. This allows teens to smoke marijuana without the smell, because e-cigarettes are a smokeless system. Either a conduction method, in which marijuana is heated by being in direct contact with something hot, or a convection method, in which hot air is blown over the marijuana to heat it, is used in e-cigarettes. E-cigarettes heat up the marijuana but do not cause it to combust. Instead, the e-cigarettes cause the essential oils, which contain the active ingredients of marijuana, to boil until an odorless vapor is created. This

Electronic cigarettes are popular with smokers trying to cut down on tobacco use or simply eliminate the smoke emissions from traditional cigarettes. Teen marijuana users have found that they can mask their habit by replacing the nicotine with marijuana and still produce an odorless aerosol discharge.

vapor can then be inhaled, and users achieve the same effect as smoking it.

Vapor pens, available at grocery stores or smoke shops, are another means of getting high from marijuana. Vapor pens look like pens used for writing but work much like e-cigarettes—heating the marijuana without producing smoke. Marijuana is placed inside the pen; users then bite on it to inhale the marijuana vapor. Students have discovered they can use vapor pens in school because they look like real pens and do not emit an odor. "I've seen people in my math class and they'll be sitting there with the teacher and they'll be smoking it and they [the teachers] won't even know,"[12] said Jack Maestas, a student at Lakewood High School in Denver, Colorado.

Skirting the Law

Although several forms of synthetic marijuana were made illegal in 2011, producers are still able to sidestep the law. Producers of synthetic marijuana create chemical compositions that produce the same effects as THC but contain slightly different ingredients than those that are listed as illegal. "These people that are making this, they're skirting the law because some of these ingredients were banned so they'll leave those out and then they'll add something else," said Vancouver police officer Jeff Starks. Manufacturers change the ingredients slightly and then sell their products as potpourri, incense, bath salts, or other things that can be legally sold. Teens buy these products and then smoke them.

Quoted in Joe Douglass, "Synthetic Pot, 'Spice,' Skirts Law Because of Changing Ingredients, Police Say," KATU, June 18, 2014. www.katu.com.

Synthetic Marijuana

Another form of marijuana is synthetic marijuana, which does not come from the marijuana plant. Instead, chemicals are mixed to create a drug that resembles marijuana but often has far more potency than the THC that occurs naturally in the marijuana plant. Because synthetic marijuana contains any number of substances and chemicals, it usually produces different, and more dangerous, effects than natural marijuana. Many users of synthetic marijuana experience seizures and psychosis, often strong enough to land them in hospital emergency rooms. Synthetic marijuana frequently consists of herbs or other leafy materials that are sprayed with chemicals that produce a high. Brightly colored, fragrant packets of synthetic marijuana are sold under various names, including Spice and K2. Users roll joints, make blunts, use bongs, or cook edibles using the synthetic marijuana, just like natural marijuana.

Spice first surfaced in 2008 and quickly became popular among high schoolers because of its legal status. Until 2011 it was legally available online, in convenience stores, and at smoke shops. When Dre was sixteen, she knew of students at school who purchased synthetic marijuana from convenience stores. She did not need to buy it to try it, because she had many friends with stashes of synthetic marijuana. Dre decided to try it, because it did not seem dangerous and it was not illegal at the time. "When you're doing it, nobody can tell you it's bad, because you'll just end up making excuses to keep smoking it," she said. "'Because it's not smoking cigarettes. Because it's not smoking weed. Because it was legal."[13]

The federal government outlawed some varieties of synthetic marijuana in 2012 under the Synthetic Drug Abuse Prevention Act. The law permanently placed twenty-six types of synthetic cannabinoids—psychoactive herbal and chemical products that mimic the effects of cannabis—and cathinones—products that have amphetamine-like properties—into Schedule I of the Controlled Substances Act. Schedule I substances, which also include heroin and LSD, are illegal to sell or use. The makers of synthetic marijuana often evade these legal restrictions by substituting different, legal chemicals in their mixtures.

Despite government efforts to continually update the list of banned cannabinoids, these drugs are still fairly easy for teens to obtain. In 2013, for instance, 7.9 percent of twelfth graders, 7.4 percent of tenth graders, and 4.0 percent of eighth graders admitted to using synthetic marijuana. The problem is that some formulations of synthetic marijuana are still technically legal, and many teens mistakenly believe that because they are legal they must be safe.

> "Young people are being harmed when they smoke these dangerous 'fake pot' products and wrongly equate the products 'legal' retail availability with being 'safe.'"[14]
>
> —Michele Leonhart, administrator of the Drug Enforcement Administration.

"Young people are being harmed when they smoke these dangerous 'fake pot' products and wrongly equate the products 'legal' retail availability with being 'safe,'"[14] said Michele Leonhart, administrator of the Drug Enforcement Administration.

More Popular than Alcohol and Cigarettes

Both synthetic marijuana and regular marijuana have become increasingly popular over the past decade, despite other substance use declining. Teen alcohol and cigarette use have actually decreased over the past decade, while marijuana use has increased. According to the 2013 National Survey on Drug Use and Health, between 2002 and 2013, teens' rate of regular alcohol use declined from 17.6 percent to 11.6 percent. Additionally, the US Department of Health and Human Services says that tobacco use among twelfth graders declined from 25 percent in 1997 to 9 percent in 2013. Meanwhile, according to the 2013 Monitoring the Future survey, overall marijuana use among teens increased. For example, 22.7 percent of twelfth graders in 2013 admitted to using marijuana in the month prior to the survey, compared to 19.4 percent in 2008. Washington State, which surveyed two hundred thousand middle and high school students in 2012, had similar findings. Students who took part in that survey were twice as likely to smoke marijuana than cigarettes. The survey also found that fewer students are using alcohol, compared to 2010.

Researchers conclude that the decrease in alcohol and cigarette use is due to awareness campaigns and that the lack of such campaigns for marijuana is why its use has increased. "More adolescents reducing their use of tobacco is an indicator, as I see it, of the effectiveness of well-funded, science-based education," said Roger Roffman, a University of Washington professor emeritus of social work and a private practice therapist. "If that can work with tobacco, why wouldn't it work with regard to marijuana?"[15]

Many teens agree that they often learn about dangers associated with alcohol and cigarettes at home and in school, but marijuana is rarely addressed. According to students, most of the health programs and interventions focus on alcohol and cigarettes. "I just hear a lot of dangers of cancer and cigarettes and I think that's why a lot of teens look to marijuana,"[16] says a Philadelphia high school junior named Tianda.

Who Is Using?

According to statistics, older teens are more likely to experiment with marijuana than younger teens. In 2013, according to the Monitoring the Future study, 22.7 percent of twelfth graders and 18 percent of tenth graders used marijuana in the month before being surveyed. This contrasts with the 7 percent of eighth graders who used marijuana in the month before the survey. The different levels of use in these age groups may be related to the ease of obtaining marijuana. Older teens are more likely to have friends who are old enough to legally obtain marijuana (in states where it is legal). These friends can then share it or sell it. "Making it legal makes it much more accessible, more available,"[17] says NIDA director Volkow. According to the 2013 Monitoring the Future study, 81 percent of twelfth graders each year have said that they could get marijuana fairly easily or very easily if they wanted some. Marijuana is not quite as easy for younger adolescents to obtain; even so, 39 percent of eighth graders and 70 percent of tenth graders say they can get marijuana if they want to.

> "I just hear a lot of dangers of cancer and cigarettes and I think that's why a lot of teens look to marijuana."[16]
>
> —*Tianda, a Pennsylvania high school junior.*

Another trend is that males are often more likely to experiment with marijuana than females. In 2013 daily marijuana use rates among twelfth graders were 8.9 percent for males versus 3.8 percent for females. Some female teens claim it is their boyfriends who lead them to marijuana.

While a freshman in high school, Jess met a boy who became her boyfriend, and with his influence, she experimented with marijuana. She says:

He was a cute soccer player, and I felt cool to have a senior looking at me. He was always saying nice things to me, and I totally fell for him. After about seven months of dating, we went to a party and I walked outside and saw him smoking pot. I was shocked: I thought he didn't want to do drugs because he was such a big athlete. But then he asked, "Would you do it with me?" I wasn't the kind of girl who did drugs, but I liked the idea of doing something new with him, and I was so into him that I didn't want to say no. So I agreed. After that, we started smoking together occasionally.[18]

Jess went on to become a regular user, even after the two broke up. She dropped out of activities and failed classes. Eventually, she decided to stop using after realizing the negative effects on her life.

Statistics also show that marijuana use is more prevalent among some ethnic groups. In 2013, according to the Monitoring the Future Study, a higher percentage of Hispanic students used marijuana compared to Caucasian and African American students in all grades surveyed. However, the percentages of Caucasian and African American students who used were

Statistics show that more boys than girls experiment with marijuana. However, many teen girls take up marijuana use because their boyfriends introduce them to the habit.

comparatively close. Caucasian students have the lowest rate of marijuana use in eighth and tenth grades, but the second highest in twelfth grade. African American students have the second highest in eighth and tenth grades but are very close to Caucasians in twelfth grade.

Another factor in determining marijuana use is whether or not a student is involved in extracurricular activities at school such as cheerleading, band, or student council or in outside organizations such as club soccer or church youth groups. In a Connecticut study of high school students, the factor most strongly associated with lower rate of marijuana use was participation in extracurricular activities. Compared to those who were involved in extracurricular activities, both girls and boys who were not involved in such activities were more likely to use marijuana: Uninvolved girls were nearly 50 percent more likely to use marijuana, and uninvolved boys were more than 25 percent more likely to use marijuana. "There are so many benefits to sports and other extracurricular activities, such as music, a church group, dance and the arts, or even volunteering, all of which can help teens avoid drug use and addiction,"[19] writes Clay Zeigler of New Beginnings Adolescent Recovery Center.

Future Use

All trends indicate that teen marijuana use is likely to continue to rise. This is mainly due to the legalization of marijuana for medical and recreational use among adults. Although it is still illegal for teens to use marijuana except in certain medical cases, the changing legal status of marijuana has led to a perception that marijuana is less risky than it actually is for teens. Also, legalization has resulted in its being easier for teens to obtain marijuana, especially through older friends. For these reasons, experts see marijuana use continuing to increase among teens.

Chapter Two

Major Influences

Many different influences can lead to a teen's decision to experiment with marijuana. These influences can range from the perception that marijuana is harmless to pressure from friends. Often, teens deal with multiple influences at once. As a result, in the past decade there has been a rising number of teens who have decided to try marijuana.

Without Risk?

One major reason that marijuana has gained popularity among teens is the perception that it carries no risks. Teens' perception of marijuana's risk has decreased over the past decade. According to the 2013 National Survey on Drug Use and Health, the percentage of twelfth graders who perceived great risk in smoking marijuana once or twice a week decreased from 54.6 percent in 2007 to 39.5 percent in 2013. Additionally, trends show that as the perception of risk decreases, use increases.

A main reason for this perception is the increasing number of states that have legalized marijuana for medical and/or recreational purposes. Many teens equate marijuana being legal to marijuana being safe for use. Under federal law the sale, possession, and use of marijuana is illegal, but many states have gone their own way in deciding the legal status of marijuana. As of January 2015 twenty-three states and Washington, DC, had enacted laws allowing the medical use of marijuana, and four states had legalized its use for recreational purposes. Joining Colorado and Washington, which previously legalized recreational marijuana, Alaska, Oregon, and Washington, DC, voted to legalize the recreational use of marijuana in the 2014 elections (although the DC vote was subject to congressional review).

With few exceptions, the changes in marijuana's legal status apply only to adults. This is similar to laws regulating who can legally drink alcohol; the consumption of alcoholic beverages is legal in all US states *only* for adults. Likewise, in all US states, marijuana is considered an illegal substance for teens except when a doctor has prescribed it for a specific medical need. Recreational marijuana remains illegal for anyone under twenty-one, no matter the circumstances.

Changing Perceptions

Police around the country are observing the effects of legalized marijuana on the actions and attitudes of youth populations. Tim O'Connell, the deputy police chief in Billings, Montana, stated in 2012 that his department was seeing an increase in marijuana use in the schools, which he attributed to the legalization of medical marijuana. Other officers have found that not only do young people today see marijuana as *not* harmful, some even consider it to be beneficial. This is the experience of Salt Lake City, Utah, police officer Doug Teerlink, who has fourteen years of experience in the police department. In his current position as a school resource officer, Teerlink encounters many teens who use marijuana and synthetic marijuana in the schools. He attributes their use of marijuana to changing perceptions. "You talk to the kids and with everything that's going on with it being legalized in Colorado and comments being made that it's just not that bad for you, the kids are taking it one step further," Teerlink stated, "and they're telling me, 'It's just an herb. It's OK. In fact, it's used for medical purposes, it's not bad for you. It's good for you.' And that's the belief that our kids are getting."[20]

Statistics supporting Teerlink's view include a 2012 Washington State Healthy Youth Survey. This survey reported that fewer Washington students in grades eight, ten, and twelve perceive a great risk of harm in using marijuana regularly. Specifically, among tenth graders, the view that marijuana is risky dropped from 65 percent in 2000 to 46 percent in 2012, the year that recreational use of marijuana became legal in Washington.

Some teens, however, see marijuana use by their peers differently. They do not believe that the legal status of marijuana is the primary force behind decisions to try the drug. "The kids who are going to use it are already using it, whether it's legal or not,"[21] said Alex Zhang, a seventeen-year-old junior at Lincoln High School in Portland, Oregon. Zhang agreed that it might be easier to get marijuana once it becomes legal. On the other hand, he adds, it is not difficult now for teens to obtain marijuana if and when they want it.

Some statistics support the view that legalization does not necessarily inspire increased use among teens. CDC researchers, for instance, have found that high school students in states that have legalized medical marijuana are only marginally more likely to have used the drug than those in states that had not

The Colorado state capitol dome rises in the background of a 2013 marijuana use holiday held in a downtown park. The previous year, Colorado and Washington became the first states to legalize marijuana use for recreational purposes.

taken this action. Additionally, in Colorado, where marijuana is legal for adult recreational use, a survey found that there was actually a small decrease in teenage use after marijuana became legal. According to Colorado's 2011 biennial Healthy Kids Colorado Survey, about 22 percent of high school students admitted to using pot in the month before the survey. The same survey done in 2013, a year after marijuana became legal in Colorado, found that number to be slightly lower, at 20 percent.

> "The kids who are going to use it are already using it, whether it's legal or not."[21]
>
> —Alex Zhang, a seventeen-year-old high school student in Oregon.

Easier Access

Even before states started legalizing marijuana for medical or recreational use, the drug was fairly common on high school campuses throughout the United States. Research shows it is now easier than ever for teens to buy it. The 2012 National Survey on American Attitudes on Substance Abuse found that 60 percent of high school students surveyed went to school where drugs were sold on campus, and 91 percent said that marijuana was the drug sold. According to Christina Zidow, chief operating officer of Odyssey House of Utah, a nonprofit substance abuse treatment facility, "It's incredibly easy to access marijuana in the school. Most of the kids in high school could find marijuana in a couple of hours if they wanted to."[22]

Although medical marijuana laws are intended to make the drug available only for legitimate medical needs, both teens and adults have found ways around these laws. One way that teens are able to obtain marijuana is by using medical marijuana cards or getting marijuana from people they know who have cards. Teens aged eighteen and nineteen are able to obtain a medical marijuana card if they can find a doctor to write them a prescription. Some younger teens have older friends who use their cards to obtain marijuana and then share it with or sell it to others.

Twenty-three states and the District of Columbia have enacted laws that permit certain patients to use marijuana for medical purposes. Some critics fear that these laws can be exploited by young people who acquire prescriptions for medical marijuana or know someone who has a prescription.

To receive a medical marijuana card, people must fill out an application in a state where medical marijuana is legal and include a doctor's recommendation with the application. Teens and adults have discovered that some doctors are quite lenient about providing a recommendation. Some doctors just question a person for a few minutes, and after being told that the person is experiencing insomnia or anxiety, the doctor issues a certificate recommending marijuana for them. Grant Glidewell, a teen drug and alcohol counselor and founder of Pacific Treatment Services in Escondido, California, explained that the teens he has counseled have easily obtained medical marijuana cards. "The most common thing I hear from kids is that they go in and say they're anxious and can't sleep,"[23] Glidewell said. Then they are given a recommendation for a prescription and are able to obtain cards.

Apparently, this method of getting a card is working. The Washington State Healthy Youth Survey found that 39 percent of high school students who used marijuana at the time of the survey said they got the drug from a medical marijuana dispensary. Some of these teens choose to share it with or even sell it to their friends. Paul Weatherly, an addiction counselor in Washington, works with addicted teens. He says his clients talk about obtaining a medical marijuana card (sometimes called a green card) and then share the drug with friends. "I ask, 'How many of you people have green cards and share with people who don't?' And they look at me like I'm the dumbest guy in [the] world. For them, it's a no-brainer,"[24] said Weatherly.

Celebrity Influence

The ease of getting the drug is just one of the factors that influence teens who choose to experiment with marijuana. Some teens are also influenced by the public comments and behavior of celebrities, especially those who have a lot of teen appeal. Performers such as Miley Cyrus, Lady Gaga, Justin Timberlake, Justin Bieber, Rihanna, Seth Rogen, and Kristen Stewart have been vocal about their marijuana use. Stewart has said that smoking marijuana is not a big deal, and Timberlake has commented that some people are better when using marijuana. Rihanna has even posted several pictures of herself smoking pot on Instagram, where millions of followers can see them. And according to Rogen, "I smoke a lot of weed when I write, generally speaking. I don't know if it helps me write. It makes me not mind that I'm writing."[25]

> "Most of the kids in high school could find marijuana in a couple of hours if they wanted to."[22]
>
> —*Christina Zidow, chief operating officer of Odyssey House of Utah.*

For some teens, seeing and hearing celebrities publicly discuss their pot use adds to its appeal. The celebrities portray using marijuana as a fun, harmless activity that has no negative effect on their lives. However, adults worry that impressionable young fans will copy these celebrities' actions. In May 2014 two members of the British pop music boy band One Direction were caught on video smoking a joint, and a picture of this was posted on the Internet. Avalon Deltaya worries that these images will influence young fans, including her younger sister. "It's an extremely bad example, my little sister loves them and I wouldn't want her copying off of them,"[26] Deltaya stated.

Peer Pressure

In addition to celebrity influence, the attitudes of friends and classmates can be major factors in a teen's decision to experiment with marijuana. Peer pressure is often at the heart of first-time use. Many teens have trouble saying no to their friends because they want to fit in. In Australia, Melbourne University's Melbourne Institute surveyed four thousand fourteen-year-olds at fifty secondary schools and found that for every one of their close friends that used marijuana, the likelihood that the teen used cannabis increased by four percentage points.

> "Everyone I looked up to was doing it. I never fit in with a group, and I saw it as an opportunity to fit in. And it was."[27]
>
> —Aaron, a teen marijuana smoker.

Aaron is an example of what can happen when teens search for ways to fit in with a group. He started using marijuana as a teenager in hopes of being accepted by his peers. "Everyone I looked up to was doing it. I never fit in with a group, and I saw it as an opportunity to fit in. And it was,"[27] says Aaron. His initial experimentation led to frequent use—and it consumed him. He was eventually suspended from school after officials caught him with a pipe and lighter on campus.

In addition to fitting in, when teens see other teens use marijuana, they often view those teens as being relaxed, enjoying themselves, and having fun. "It seems cool to people," said junior Chris Maurice when asked why he believes teens are drawn to pot. "Kids see people that smoke weed who seem to be pret-

Parental Approval Not Required

In Washington, if older teens are able to find a doctor to write them a medical marijuana prescription, they can obtain marijuana without their parents' permission or knowledge.

In 2014 a Washington parent discovered that her eighteen-year-old son had been expelled from high school for selling marijuana to other students. She learned that her son had legally obtained a medical marijuana card without her knowledge. She has no idea how or why a doctor would have prescribed marijuana for her son. He ultimately used his card to buy marijuana that he ended up selling to other students.

ty happy with their lives."[28] When certain teens see others like this, it appeals to them and creates a desire to try it themselves.

A New Type of Pressure

In the past decade a new type of pressure has affected teens' decisions regarding marijuana and other drugs. Social media and other forms of entertainment now take up much of the average teenager's day. Social media, including Twitter, Instagram, and Facebook, have become a great influence on teens and the choices they make. Studies show that 25 percent of teens log in to social media ten-plus times per day. According to a study of eight- to eighteen-year-olds conducted by the Kaiser Family Foundation, today's teens spend more than 7.5 hours a day with various forms of media, including watching TV, listening to music, surfing the web, social networking, and playing video games.

During their online time, many teens are influenced by what they see and read. This is the finding of a 2012 study conducted by the National Center on Addiction and Substance Abuse at Columbia University (CASAColumbia). In that study,

75 percent of twelve- to seventeen-year-olds said that seeing pictures of teens partying with alcohol or marijuana on social networking sites such as Facebook or MySpace encourages them to party in the same way. The same survey found that 45 percent of teens have seen online pictures of teens using drugs, and 47 percent of those teens said that it seemed like the pictured teens were having a good time. The study also found that teens who have seen these pictures were found to be four times more likely to have used marijuana than those who had not viewed these types of images online. "Digital peer pressure moves beyond a child's friends and the kids they hang out with. It invades the home and a child's bedroom via the Internet,"[29] Joseph A. Califano Jr., founder and chair emeritus of CASAColumbia, said.

Social media has also been used by teens to sell and buy drugs such as marijuana. Various social media let users post pictures with hashtags and captions. Drug dealers have used these types of social media to advertise their goods with full-color pictures. Some dealers list their cell phone number or e-mail address along with the pictures, but many use various messaging apps, which provide relatively anonymous messaging without using phone numbers or other self-identifying information. "There is some secret language, but for the most part you can hashtag 'marijuana', hashtag 'Xanax', any drug you can think of, you can find that on social media,"[30] said Constance Phillips, the admissions manager for Houston's Odyssey House, a drug treatment facility for teenagers. Certain hashtags or search keywords allow kids to easily find what they are looking for and make a deal to buy the drugs.

Dealing with Life

In addition to peer and digital pressure, dealing with difficulties in life can lead teens to marijuana. Issues such as divorce, death, moving, and other major life changes can cause a high level of stress in teens. This type of stress can result in a per-

Teens are faced with stress at home and at school. The pressure to succeed academically or athletically can overwhelm teens, leading some to seek relief in marijuana use.

son seeking relief, and in some cases marijuana is perceived as a way to relieve that stress.

Seeking relief, teens like Jessica have turned to marijuana during times of struggle in their lives. After her parents divorced, she lived with her mom, who was stressed herself trying to make a living. This resulted in major stress in Jessica's life. She said:

> My mom had a tough time making ends meet after my parents divorced when I was 14. She was always picking big fights with me over little things because she was so stressed. One weekend, I went to my friend's house to escape my mom's mood, and some kids were smoking pot. I thought it was harmless, so I took a puff. And within minutes, I felt a wave of relief; I smiled for the first time in months.[31]

For a while marijuana brought Jessica escape and relief, but then it no longer did. In fact, it actually added to her stress. Eventually, after realizing it really did not help her deal with her problems, Jessica was able to stop using marijuana.

Mental illness can also be a reason that teens turn to marijuana. Teens who deal with depression or other mental illnesses often seek relief through marijuana and other drugs. One Office of National Drug Control Policy study found that depressed youths are more than twice as likely to have used or become dependent on marijuana as youths who do not suffer from depression.

Self-medicating, the term used by health professionals to describe turning to drugs for relief from problems, does not usually resolve those problems. If anything, it can make them worse. Lydia Shrier, a doctor with the division of adolescent and young adult medicine at Boston Children's Hospital, has seen many teens who use marijuana to cope with depression and other personal issues. The initial high they feel can seem to be an improvement, but that feeling does not usually last. Shrier explained, "People feel bad, they use, and they might momen-

> "I thought it was harmless, so I took a puff. And within minutes, I felt a wave of relief; I smiled for the first time in months."[31]
>
> —Jessica, who started smoking marijuana at age fourteen.

Tending Toward Risk

"Didn't you think about the consequences?" This question is probably familiar to many teens. It is the kind of question parents ask when they find out their teenager has done something that they think was obviously not a good idea, such as not studying for a test, sneaking out in the middle of the night to meet with a friend, or getting drunk or high at a party. In answer to that question, many teens would probably say no, they did not think about the consequences.

Teens are not hard-wired to fully consider consequences when making decisions. Studies have actually found that because teens' brains are not fully developed, they are more likely to take risks and less likely to control their impulses. "Teenagers are not as readily able to access their frontal lobe to say, 'Oh, I better not do this,'" says neuroscientist Frances Jensen. This is why, when presented with a decision such as whether or not to try marijuana, teens are more inclined than adults to partake. Even if they know the possible consequences, their impulsivity may override their judgment about what might be the best choice in any given situation.

Quoted in *Fresh Air*, "Why Teens Are Impulsive, Addiction-Prone, and Should Protect Their Brains," NPR, January 28, 2015. www.npr.org.

tarily feel better, but then they feel worse. They don't necessarily link feeling bad after using with the use itself, so it can become a vicious cycle."[32]

Medical Conditions

Other teens have turned to marijuana to help them deal with medical conditions, even when they have not received a medical marijuana card with a doctor's recommendation. In some of these cases, their parents have approved of this use, despite the fact it is illegal and potentially dangerous.

Joanie suffered a skiing injury at age thirteen; a rod inserted in her knee caused her extreme pain. At the time, her doctors prescribed a variety of painkillers, but she developed stomach problems and depression. A few years later she had another surgery because her leg grew and she needed a longer rod; this also resulted in great pain and more prescribed painkillers. At sixteen she suffered whiplash in a car accident, causing even more pain. The painkillers prescribed for her caused numerous side effects, including migraines. Joanie heard that marijuana could be used to reduce chronic pain. When she tried it she found that it significantly reduced her pain, and she was able to get off the other medications. "I could tell instantly that it made me feel a lot better: it took my mind off the pain, and made me less depressed,"[33] stated Joanie. Now eighteen, she has a legal card and uses marijuana every day.

Many doctors have issues with teens using marijuana to deal with chronic pain. The Mayo Clinic, a well-respected hospital research and treatment center, has studied the effects of marijuana for chronic pain management among teens and does not recommend its use. According to the Mayo Clinic, although marijuana may help teens with some specific conditions related to chronic pain, its adverse effects, even with short-term use, can include fatigue, impaired concentration, and slower reaction times.

Another medical issue that teens deal with is attention-deficit/hyperactivity disorder (ADHD), which causes inattentiveness and difficulty maintaining focus. Some teens and their parents claim that marijuana has helped alleviate the teens' ADHD symptoms. Certain doctors have even prescribed medical marijuana for teens with ADHD because they agree that it is helpful. However, other health professionals think this is a dangerous idea. "The active ingredient in pot, THC, causes short term memory problems and inattention," stated Stephen Hinshaw, a professor of psychology at the University of California at Berkeley, "the very same things you want a medicine for ADHD to eliminate."[34]

For a variety of reasons, more teens are turning to marijuana and using it as a part of their daily lives. Every day teens are faced with different pressures and other factors that push them toward experimenting with marijuana. Often, when facing the pressures, it is difficult for teens to make wise choices regarding marijuana use.

Chapter Three

The Consequences of Marijuana Use

At some point in their teen years, many of today's youth face a choice: whether or not to use marijuana. Although for the most part it is illegal for teens to buy or use marijuana in all fifty US states, most teens say they can easily get it if they want it. Consequently, health professionals and others try to encourage young people to think carefully about the possible consequences of using marijuana before they try it. Among those who have spoken out publicly about teens and marijuana is President Barack Obama, who is the father of two teenage girls. "I view it as a bad habit and a vice, not very different from the cigarettes that I smoked as a young person up through a big chunk of my adult life," Obama said during an interview for an article in the *New Yorker*. Obama added that he has explained to his own daughters that he thinks smoking marijuana is "a bad idea, a waste of time, not very healthy."[35]

Understanding the Effects of Marijuana

The difficulty in getting teens to listen to advice about marijuana, whether it comes from the president or from a member of their own family, is that many teens know people who have smoked marijuana without disastrous results. Friends and sometimes even parents have amusing stories to tell about their days of smoking pot. Anecdotal stories such as these might be fun to tell or hear, but they should not be confused with facts. The widespread and growing use of marijuana, both for recreational and medical purposes, has inspired a wave of medical research in which scientists seek to better understand the physical and emotional effects of marijuana.

One area of recent research involves examining the effects of marijuana on specific body organs and systems. Recent research shows, for example, that smoking pot can increase a user's heart rate by as much as two times for up to three hours after smoking. This increases a person's risk of a heart attack. A 2014 study from Boston's Beth Israel Deaconess Medical Center and Harvard Medical School found that marijuana increases the risk of having a heart attack within the first hour of smoking to five times that of nonsmokers.

The long-term physical effects of marijuana are unclear at this time. Some studies link marijuana smoking to increased chance of lung cancer or emphysema, similar to smoking cigarettes, but other studies dispute this. Other studies have found that long-term marijuana use can weaken a person's immune system, but the studies are too small in scope to be definitive. Several ongoing studies seek to determine if regular marijuana use has long-term repercussions, and if so, how serious they might be.

The Brain

Health professionals' greatest concern regarding teens and marijuana involves the possible effects of marijuana on the brain. A person's brain is not fully developed until he or she is about twenty-five years old. Until that point, mind-altering substances can potentially change the brain's development. Recent studies support the theory that using marijuana as a teen can negatively affect the brain.

At the 2014 American Psychological Association's annual convention, Krista Lisdahl, director of the brain imaging and neuropsychology lab at the University of Wisconsin at Milwaukee, discussed the results of studies that looked at the effects of marijuana on the teenage brain. According to Lisdahl, a growing number of studies of teens who use marijuana at least once a week show that this use actually changes the structure of the brain. What researchers saw on the brain images of sixteen- to eighteen-year-old marijuana users were abnormalities in the brain's gray matter. This is the area associated with intelligence.

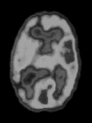
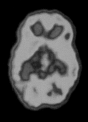
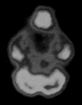

NORMAL

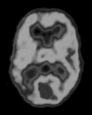
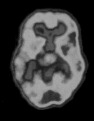
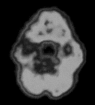

MARIJUANA ABUSER

The brain scans of a non–marijuana user (top) and a marijuana abuser (bottom) show marked differences. Red areas of high brain activity almost disappear in the cerebellum (at the far right) of the marijuana user, typically resulting in poor coordination and impaired spatial judgment.

The specific areas in the brain that changed are those that deal with memory and problem solving. Lisdahl said the studies found cognitive decline, poor attention and memory, and decreased IQ in those who had started smoking pot regularly before age twenty-five. "It needs to be emphasized that regular cannabis use, defined here as once a week, is not safe and may result in addiction and neurocognitive damage, especially in youth,"[36] said Lisdahl in a study she cowrote that was published in the June 2014 issue of the journal *Current Addiction Reports*.

Results of Brain Change

These brain changes may end up negatively affecting a person's memory and intellectual abilities. Studies have found a link between declining IQ and regular marijuana use. A 2012 study published in the *Proceedings of the National Academy of Sciences* included more than one thousand people. Their IQ was tested at ages thirteen and thirty-eight, and they were asked about marijuana use between those ages. The study found that people who had become addicted to marijuana before age eighteen lost an average of eight IQ points by adulthood. According to study author Madeline Meier, a professor at Arizona State University, even teens who eventually quit marijuana may have irrevocably reduced their IQ. "Regular teen cannabis users who stopped using later in life, by adulthood, they still showed IQ decline, so quitting use as an adult didn't result in recovery of IQ function,"[37] stated Meier.

> "We observed that the shapes of brain structures related to short-term memory seemed to collapse inward or shrink in people who had a history of daily marijuana use."[38]
>
> —Matthew Smith, assistant research professor in psychiatry and behavioral sciences at Northwestern University Feinberg School of Medicine.

Studies have also found that memory may be affected by marijuana use. A 2013 study conducted by Northwestern University Feinberg School of Medicine researchers, reported in the journal *Schizophrenia Bulletin*, found brain abnormalities and memory problems in chronic marijuana smokers. Participants in the study, all in their early twenties, were tested two years after they had stopped smoking marijuana. During testing, researchers saw shrinkage in the parts of the brain that control memory. "We observed that the shapes of brain structures related to short-term memory seemed to collapse inward or shrink in people who had a history of daily marijuana use when compared to healthy participants,"[38] said Matthew Smith, study author and assistant research professor in psychiatry and behavioral sciences at Northwestern University Feinberg School of Medicine. Researchers also noticed more abnormalities in the brains of participants who started using marijuana at a younger age.

Edible Overdose

As with other drugs, there is more than one way to consume marijuana. But few drugs other than marijuana find their way into food. Edibles that contain marijuana (either parts of the plant or oil) have become popular with people who use the drug for medical reasons. Marijuana that is eaten is slower to take effect than marijuana that is smoked, but the effects last longer—a benefit for people who use the drug to relieve pain and other symptoms of illness. The benefits of eating versus smoking marijuana have not been lost on those who use the drug for nonmedical reasons. As a result, the market for edible marijuana products has grown—and teens are among those who are sampling these products.

Health officials in some states are seeing a rise in the number of overdose cases involving marijuana edibles. Many of these cases involve children and teenagers. The primary problem is that users often eat more than the suggested serving size

Serving-Size Math

It is hard to eat just one. This is true of cookies, candy, and many treats that are now sold as marijuana edibles. The problem with marijuana edibles is that eating more than one serving is dangerous and not eating more than one serving requires restraint. In Colorado, a single serving of an edible purchased for recreational use can contain up to 10 milligrams of THC but a single package or product can include as many as ten servings. This means a bag of marijuana gummies, a marijuana chocolate bar, or a marijuana brownie can contain as much as 100 milligrams of THC. In contrast, a single puff on a marijuana cigarette transfers to the user about 5 milligrams of THC. So, eating all ten gummies in a bag of marijuana candy, with each gummy classified as a single 10-milligram serving, would be the equivalent of twenty hits of a marijuana cigarette at one time. This explains why the chance of overdose is so high when teens get their hands on marijuana edibles.

because the cookie or brownie or other product tastes good and does not appear to be having any effect. "With edibles, children and teens may consume higher quantities than the inhaled form. It takes much longer for the THC to go through the gut than to be inhaled, so a teen may not experience a 'high' which leads to eating more and more,"[39] stated Dr. Yolanda Evans, an adolescent expert at Seattle Children's Hospital. The result of eating more than the recommended amount can be quite dangerous, potentially even requiring hospitalization.

Since Colorado legalized marijuana for recreational use, hospitals there have seen an increase in people being admitted for edible overdose. Dr. Richard Zane of the University of Colorado Hospital in Denver has said that the hospital is admitting about one person a day for pot-related problems, and most are linked to edibles. Many people experiencing adverse marijuana effects arrive in the emergency room with symptoms such as nausea, elevated heart rate, anxiety, and hallucinations. "You have college students who are pretty naive who are sucking on a THC-infused lollipop and are psychotic for two or three days because they've never had this level of THC or this strength,"[40] said Zane.

In 2014 five Northern California teenagers experienced the dangerous results that edibles can produce. The teens, who were students at De Anza High School, fell ill after eating marijuana brownies that they bought from another student. Two of the students were unconscious and were rushed to the hospital, while the other three were treated at the school for dizziness and vomiting. In this case all of the students recovered, and the school disciplined the student who sold the marijuana.

Synthetic Marijuana Risks

Just as edibles have increased in popularity, so has the use of synthetic marijuana—especially among youth. Synthetic marijuana entered the market in the early 2000s, and it became popular quickly as teens realized that they could purchase synthetic marijuana legally. Synthetic marijuana products contain dried, shredded plant materials that are sprayed with chemical additives; these additives are responsible for psychoactive

Initially a legal alternative to marijuana, Spice was composed of plant fibers combined with synthetic chemicals that produced the same high. However, because of medical problems associated with synthetic marijuana use, Spice was banned by the Synthetic Drug Abuse Prevention Act of 2012.

mind-altering effects like those produced by marijuana's THC. However, there are major differences between synthetic marijuana and natural marijuana; studies are finding that synthetic marijuana is much more toxic and more dangerous than natural marijuana. A recent Boston University School of Medicine study found that synthetic marijuana causes increased risk of paranoia and panic in users.

In fact, poison control centers around the country have seen a spike in calls related to the effects of synthetic marijuana. According to a 2012 study published in the journal *Pediatrics*, the American Association of Poison Control Centers received forty-five hundred calls involving problems from synthetic marijuana from 2010 to 2011. In one instance a sixteen-year-old girl had her eyes open but was not responding to verbal or physical cues to get her attention. In another case an eighteen-year-old boy called in because he was agitated and sweating excessively. A third case involved a sixteen-year-old boy who entered an emergency room hallucinating and with slow speech.

> "The high is great, but in the long run, it isn't good. It's no fun to be stuck in a wheelchair, to have to go to therapy or (possibly) die."[41]
>
> —Emily Bauer, a seventeen-year-old synthetic marijuana user.

Seventeen-year-old Emily Bauer has experienced devastating effects from synthetic marijuana. In December 2012 Emily was hospitalized after suffering several strokes that left her paralyzed, blind, and on life support. She had been using synthetic marijuana daily prior to the hospitalization. Emily developed vasculitis, which is an inflammation of the blood vessels, that limited the blood and oxygen flow to her brain. She was out of school for nine months during this period, and the damage to her brain has left her unable to read or write. "The high is great, but in the long run, it isn't good," Emily said, describing her experience smoking synthetic marijuana. "It's no fun to be stuck in a wheelchair, to have to go to therapy or (possibly) die."[41] She recovered to the point that she now lives at home and attends school, but she remains in a wheelchair and needs help with simple tasks.

Addiction Issues

Research into the effects of marijuana use is ongoing. One area being studied is addiction. There has been much debate on how addictive marijuana is. In some ways it is similar to alcohol; many people who drink alcohol can do so without developing an addiction. The same may be true for marijuana. However, studies have found that the younger a person is when he or she begins to use marijuana, the more likely that person is to develop an addiction.

The earlier a person experiments with marijuana, the higher the risk of developing an addiction. Several studies have been conducted with results that show the link between early use and increased chance of addiction. According to the National Institutes of Health, about 9 percent of people who use marijuana will become dependent on it. However, this percentage increases if a person starts using while young—about 16 percent of kids who use marijuana eventually become addicted to it. An Australian study found that daily adolescent users were eighteen times more likely to become dependent on marijuana by age thirty than those who did not start using marijuana until they were older. Researchers are unsure why this is the case, but other studies have found similar results.

Gateway Drug?

Does marijuana use lead to the use of other, more dangerous drugs? Experts are divided on whether or not using marijuana leads to increased drug experimentation—that is, whether marijuana is a gateway drug. According to the Marijuana Policy Project, a national organization working for marijuana law reform, 107 million Americans have tried marijuana, but only 37 million Americans have tried heroin. According to the Marijuana Policy Project, this proves there is no correlation between marijuana and harder drug use. The group believes that significantly more people would have tried heroin if marijuana truly was a gateway drug. On the other hand, a 2012 Yale University study, which appeared online in the *Journal of Adolescent Health*, showed that alcohol, cigarettes, and marijuana were associated with an increased likelihood of prescription drug abuse in men age eighteen to twenty-five. Additionally, in women of that age, marijuana use was linked with a higher chance of prescription drug abuse. The debate continues about whether teens who use marijuana are more likely to try drugs such as prescription pills, cocaine, or heroin.

For those who become addicted and try to stop, withdrawal symptoms similar to that of nicotine withdrawal are likely to occur. People who try to quit marijuana report difficulty sleeping and experience anxiety and irritability. Additionally, people who have tried to quit show increased aggression on psychological tests.

Greg Williams understands how hard it is to stop after addiction. At age thirteen, he began smoking marijuana and soon became hooked. "I'd wake up every morning wondering how I was going to get high," he said. "I'd smoke in the woods after school and at parties on weekends. I didn't have that shut-off switch. I would use up everything until it was gone."[42] He also developed an alcohol and prescription drug habit, and by high school he was high most of the time. His parents realized he had a problem and had Greg attend addiction counseling, but it did not help. Greg continued to use marijuana, drink, and do other drugs.

The summer after he graduated high school, Greg drove his car while under the influence of drugs, ended up running into a tree, and landed in the emergency room. After he recovered from his injuries, his parents placed him in an inpatient drug treatment program that Greg credits with turning his life around. After a month-long stay at the program, he went on to attend Quinnipiac University in Connecticut and eventually graduated with a 3.75 grade point average. He also discovered that life had a lot more to offer than a high from drugs. "I used to say there was all this stuff I was going to do, like snowboarding, bungee jumping, or going to Europe, which never happened because I was too stoned to get up off the couch," Greg said. "Now I've done it all, and more."[43]

Mental Health

Mental health issues have also surfaced as an area of interest in research being done on the consequences of teen marijuana use. Scientists in Australia and New Zealand, for instance, have identified a possible link between early marijuana use and suicidal thoughts. The researchers studied the effects of marijuana on users who started before age seventeen. Their study, published in the *Lancet Psychiatry* journal in 2014, found that teens in this group who used marijuana daily were seven times more likely to attempt suicide than nonusers. Tied to this is a 2008 Office of National Drug Control Policy study that stated weekly or more frequent use of marijuana doubles a teen's risk of depression and anxiety. Both studies indicate that teens using marijuana could have a higher chance of developing mental health issues.

The same study by researchers from Australia and New Zealand found that teens who are regular users of marijuana may lose interest in people, activities, and goals. According to the study, teens who frequently used marijuana became less motivated than those who used less frequently or not at all. Additionally, those who used marijuana daily before age seventeen were 63 percent less likely to finish high school than subjects who abstained and 62 percent less likely to earn a college degree. By comparison, subjects who smoked pot less often than monthly before age seventeen were 22 percent less likely than nonusers to finish high school and 22 percent less likely to earn a college degree. "This paper provides the best evidence to date on the harms of marijuana use during adolescence as it combines three large longitudinal studies that track the lives of children through to adulthood,"[44] stated Associate Professor Simon Denny from the Faculty of Medical and Health Sciences at the University of Auckland.

Greg Merson, who became a millionaire as a poker player in his twenties, accomplished this only after turning his life around after marijuana and other drugs interfered with his future. Merson said, "I was a straight-A student from sixth grade until I

> "I used to say there was all this stuff I was going to do, like snowboarding, bungee jumping, or going to Europe, which never happened because I was too stoned to get up off the couch."[43]
>
> —Greg Williams, a teen who underwent treatment for drug addiction.

Greg Merson poses with his winnings at the 2012 World Series of Poker Main Event in Las Vegas. Before becoming a tournament gambler, Merson was a marijuana user who kicked the habit by attending Narcotics Anonymous meetings.

graduated high school—straight edge, didn't do anything. And then as soon as I graduated high school, as soon as I got back from high school senior week, I just started smoking weed every day."[45] He went on to college, but his use increased to the point that he was barely functioning. He went from straight As in high school to a 1.1 GPA at college.

Merson realized something had to change and was able to become sober while he attended Narcotics Anonymous meetings. His motivation in life came back, and he decided to become a professional poker player. By age twenty-five, in 2014, he had earned $9 million as a poker player, which he does not believe would have happened if he had continued his drug use.

Driving Under the Influence

What draws many to marijuana is how it makes them feel re-laxed and uninhibited. However, these feelings can result in dangerous situations when a person who is high attempts to accomplish an action that requires alertness and awareness. Driving is one of these actions. When teens do decide to ex-periment with marijuana, they may find themselves having to make yet another choice: whether to drive while under the in-fluence of marijuana. Making the choice to drive can have dire consequences.

Driving under the influence of marijuana is extremely dan-gerous, as dangerous as drunk driving. This is because mari-juana slows down people's responses to sights and sounds. Also, marijuana can make a user sleepy, distort his or her sense of time and space, and hurt the person's ability to deal with changes in lighting. All of these combined make it difficult to handle the many tasks required while driving.

Many teens who use marijuana make the wise choice not to drive and do not endanger themselves and others. Howev-er, other teens choose differently. Statistics show that more than 10 percent of teens who use marijuana do decide to drive while under its influence. These teens put themselves and their passengers at risk of an accident that may harm or kill themselves or others. In 2015 the Columbia University Mailman School of Public Health released a study that sug-gested half of the teen and young adult drivers who die in car crashes are under the influence of either marijuana, alco-hol, or both. For the study, researchers used data regarding sixteen- to twenty-five-year-olds from the Fatality Analysis Reporting System, a federal database of fatal crashes. Just over half of the drivers were either drunk or high at the time of their fatal car crashes.

Adam Daszkal, eighteen, has discovered the consequenc-es of driving while under the influence of marijuana. In August 2013 Boca Raton, Florida, police arrested him for driving under the influence and causing a car accident that killed sixty-five-year-old Camil Paquet, a Canadian father of two. According to a police report, Daszkal told an officer he was under the influence of marijuana when he crashed into Paquet's motorcycle, and a blood test later confirmed this confession. Daszkal was charged with DUI manslaughter, and in January 2015 his attorney and the prosecutor agreed to a plea deal in which he received five years' probation, 250 hours of community service, a one-year driver's license suspension, and random drug and alcohol testing.

Legal Consequences

Many teens face pressure from friends to experiment with marijuana. Others are pressured into selling it. Teens who choose to sell marijuana risk legal consequences. In cities and towns across the United States, teens who chose to sell marijuana have faced serious charges—hurting themselves, their families, and their futures. Adam Kuhar, eighteen, was arrested in 2014 after police executed a search warrant at his home in Ohio. They collected more than 2 pounds (907 g) of marijuana in the home. Kuhar was facing felony charges for possessing and trafficking marijuana.

Another teen developed a highly profitable marijuana ring but soon found that he could not evade the law and had to face the consequences. In 2012 Tyler Pagenstecher, convicted of selling up to $20,000 worth of high-grade marijuana a month to high school students in southwestern Ohio, was sentenced to six months to three years in a juvenile prison. Authorities believe that Pagenstecher began selling the drugs when he was about fifteen and managed to avoid arrest for a long time by not selling the marijuana at school. Instead, he mainly sold it out of his home. After being sentenced, Pagenstecher apologized and admitted he had not realized how severe the results of his actions could be. "I understood that I would get in trouble but not to the level or extent this has become, and I sincerely regret all of this," he said. "If I could take it all back, I would."[46]

Pagenstecher learned the hard way that selling marijuana can lead to regrets. Using marijuana can also lead to regrets. Despite the fact that many people can recreationally use marijuana and suffer no adverse consequences, there is no guarantee of this for adults or teens. And studies have shown that teens are at an even greater risk than adults of experiencing the downsides of marijuana. Their choices regarding marijuana have a direct impact on their future.

Chapter Four

Reducing Teen Usage

Although teen marijuana use is on the rise, many teens actually choose not to experiment with marijuana or other drugs. Emily Knowlton has seen what marijuana has done to her friends, and she has chosen not to try it. "I saw people who I met and knew and loved and watched their lives change through marijuana. Suddenly, my friends could no longer hold conversations anymore; they jumped from topic to topic," writes Knowlton. "I saw their lives gobbled away [by] smoking; they became oblivious of everything in their lives and could only talk about marijuana, or who doesn't smoke, whose against it, how it feels, how much they bought."[47] Increasing the number of young people who decide against trying marijuana—at least in their teen years—is the goal of many societal efforts and programs. These range from laws to educational efforts—and they have had varying levels of success.

Laws and Teens

The most common method to dissuade teens from marijuana use is through the law. Although twenty-three states and Washington, DC, allow medical marijuana, and Colorado, Alaska, Oregon, and Washington allow recreational marijuana, these laws mainly apply to adults. Across the nation, it is illegal for teens to buy, sell, and/or use marijuana recreationally. Medically, only teens who qualify can use marijuana, and this qualification requires a doctor's recommendation and oversight. Many doctors are careful about prescribing medical marijuana to teens, but there are some doctors who will more easily provide a prescription. Doctors have the leeway to prescribe for conditions such as migraines or anxiety, and teens have faked these symptoms to obtain cards.

Teens who disobey the laws run the risk of punishment ranging from community service to juvenile detention or jail. What state a person lives in is one factor that determines how severe the consequences of disobeying marijuana laws are. For example, in some states possession of a small amount of marijuana will only result in a fine, whereas in other states the same crime can result in criminal charges. In Georgia any person who is found in possession of 1 ounce (28 g) or less of marijuana can face a fine of $1,000 and receive a maximum sentence of a year's incarceration. However, in Nevada if a person is found with 1 ounce or less of marijuana, the maximum fine is $600 with no jail time.

Early Awareness Campaigns

The threat of legal action does not always convince teens to abstain from marijuana. A more effective tactic, some say, is making sure teens know about the potential risks of marijuana use so that they can make better choices. Several nonprofit organizations, medical associations, and government agencies have created marijuana awareness campaigns aimed specifically at teens. The purpose of these campaigns is to discourage teens from experimenting with marijuana, or if they already have experimented, to encourage them to stop using. Many of these campaigns focus on presenting teens with research that shows that the earlier people start smoking marijuana, the greater their likelihood of becoming addicted. Additionally, these programs explain other research that shows links between early marijuana use and changes in the brain.

The awareness campaigns of an earlier era tried to use scary images to convince teens to stay away from marijuana and other drugs. For example, in 1987 the Partnership for a Drug-Free America launched its This Is Your Brain on Drugs campaign. Public service announcements showed an egg frying in a pan and equated this to what happens to people's brains when they use drugs. "The ad wasn't helpful in deterring me from using drugs. I don't think that scare tactics ever work in preventing kids from doing anything," says Taia Lubitz, who was a high school student at the time of the campaign. "I think that a scare tactic acts as more of a dare than it does actually scare kids away from using drugs."[48]

Studies since that time have shown that fear campaigns do not work. Instead, studies show that giving teens factual information so that they can make independent choices is a more effective method. For years, the organization Drug Abuse Resistance Education (D.A.R.E.) produced among the most widely known campaigns against youth drug use. One of the more famous D.A.R.E. campaigns was its Just Say No anti-drug education program that initially launched in 1983. D.A.R.E. campaigns have reached many students through programs presented in schools, but studies call into question some of the organization's tactics. According to critics, D.A.R.E. campaigns sometimes exaggerated the information they presented to teens in an effort to scare them away from marijuana and other drugs—and teens picked up on this. "Especially with teens, you've got to be credible,"[49] said Michael Slater, an anti-drug campaign expert at Ohio State University.

> **"Especially with teens, you've got to be credible."[49]**
>
> —Michael Slater, an anti-drug campaign expert at Ohio State University.

According to an article published in the *Journal of Consulting and Clinical Psychology*, D.A.R.E. did not actually reduce teenagers' experimentation with drugs. The article described a study that found that twenty-year-olds who had taken part in D.A.R.E. programs were just as likely to have succumbed to peer pressure to try marijuana and other drugs, cigarettes, and alcohol as kids who had never taken part in D.A.R.E. In response to this study, D.A.R.E. changed its message and campaign methods, but critics still say the organization's campaigns include exaggerations, and teens are able to detect these.

D.A.R.E. programs have been criticized for using scare tactics to turn kids away from drugs. Some experts believe that kids are more likely to stay clear of drugs if they are presented with credible facts rather than exaggerated statistics and frightening stories.

Slater says that giving teens choices with credible information is the most effective method to convince them not to use marijuana or other drugs. Youth agree with this method. Brittany, who started using marijuana as a seventh grader and ended up in a drug rehabilitation program at age sixteen, believes programs need to be honest with teens about marijuana. Her school had a program that focused on just saying no to drugs, but according to Brittany, never explained why. Instead of suggesting a simplistic just-say-no message, she says, campaigns need to present factual information to kids about the possible consequences of using marijuana. "I think people could make younger kids more aware of how bad it is, what it could do to you and that it is harmful,"[50] she said.

Don't Be a Lab Rat

Aware of efforts that have *not* worked, some states have implemented their own programs to discourage teens from using marijuana. Colorado, where recreational use for adults is legal, has created a program that tells young people flat out that no one knows for sure how marijuana affects teens. The campaign, Don't Be a Lab Rat, began in 2014.

The idea behind the Colorado campaign is to get teens to think about whether they want to be lab rats in an experiment—one that requires them to wait and see how marijuana will affect their brains and personalities. The program uses spots on television, website information, and displays it places in public places, such as schools. These displays include laboratory cages with oversize hamster water bottles and signs explaining the dangers of marijuana. "Schizophrenia. Permanent IQ loss. Stunted brain growth. Still, some people question this research. Claiming the studies need to go deeper. Look further. But who will be their guinea pigs?" The Don't Be a Lab Rat website asks, "Who's going to risk their brains to find out once and for all what marijuana really does?"[51]

A skateboarder investigates the giant cage used as part of a Don't Be a Lab Rat anti-marijuana campaign in Denver. This unique program uses such imagery to get teens to question whether they want to risk the unknown, long-term effects of marijuana use for short-term highs.

This campaign has provoked some controversy as certain school districts disagreed with the methods used. The Boulder Valley School District announced it would not participate in the campaign because the superintendent did not think an over-size rat cage was an appropriate prop to have in schools. However, Mike Sukle, who runs the ad agency the state hired to design the campaign, disagrees. He believes that the campaign is an honest approach that teens will be affected by when they view it. "A lot of the facts are from studies that are preliminary. And we wanted to be honest with the kids about that," Sukle says. "Maybe [marijuana] isn't going to be as bad as it looks, but it could be really damaging. The campaign asks teens whether they want to take that risk."[52]

> "Maybe [marijuana] isn't going to be as bad as it looks, but it could be really damaging. The campaign asks teens whether they want to take that risk."[52]
>
> —Mike Sukle, an ad agency head who oversees the Don't Be a Lab Rat campaign.

Drug Zombies

Some groups have turned to images from popular culture to get teens to think twice before trying marijuana. Zombies have been front and center in television and movies in recent years. The success of shows such as AMC's *The Walking Dead* has inspired district authorities in Washington, DC, to incorporate zombies into their campaign against the use of synthetic marijuana. Teens in DC have been experimenting more and more with synthetic marijuana—with dangerous results. A district survey found that the average age of a synthetic marijuana user in DC is thirteen. Officials designed a public education program with this in mind.

In 2013 the district's health department began its K2 Zombie DC campaign to warn teens that synthetic marijuana will turn them into slow, addled zombies. The campaign, which has been conducted in print and online, uses before-and-after pictures to illustrate the point. The before pictures show typical teens; the after pictures show gory zombies and include the slogan "Danger: Fake Weed + U = Zombie."

Social Media Blitz

As studies have shown, teens are affected by what they see and read on social media. This can lead them to increased drug use. However, anti-drug campaigns are now turning to social media to stop this increase. Above the Influence has run ads on Tumblr, Instagram, and Facebook. It continues to promote the message of choice, as opposed to a simple message of just saying no to drugs. "Saying 'Don't do drugs because they're bad for you' became ineffective because . . . [teens'] sense of mortality is nil," says Allen Rosenshine, vice chair and executive director of the Partnership at Drugfree.org. "It's more insightful and in tune with the target audience to say: 'Drugs rob you of yourself. You can be better than that. You have things you want to do and don't let drugs get in your way.'" These messages seem to be reaching teens; by December 2014 Above the Influence had more than 1.8 million likes.

Quoted in Stuart Elliott, "Antidrug Campaign, Lacking Federal Funds, Turns to Social Media," *New York Times*, July 15, 2013. www.nytimes.com.

Above the Influence

Whereas many programs, such K2 Zombie DC and Don't Be a Lab Rat, are state and city efforts, a campaign called Above the Influence works on a national scale. It discourages the use of marijuana and other drugs by encouraging teens to make their own decisions and not be influenced by their peers.

The program, run by Partnership for Drug-Free Kids, has used commercials, public service announcements, and print and Internet advertising to get its message out. It has also partnered with local community groups to create activities to educate teens about drugs and alcohol. The media messages and activities focus on helping teens understand the pressures that might lead them to try drugs and alcohol and helping them remain true to themselves by making their own decisions. For example, in 2014 Above the Influence encouraged teens to take a picture of themselves showing how they stay above the influence and then post it on Instagram with the hashtags #abovetheinfluence and #ATIWeek2014.

Various studies have found this program to be effective at reducing drug use among teens. A study published in the journal *Prevention Science* in 2011, for example, found that youth who reported exposure to the campaign were less likely to try marijuana than those who had no exposure to the Above the Influence campaign. This study surveyed more than three thousand students in twenty communities nationwide. It found that by the end of eighth grade, 12 percent of those who did not see or participate in the campaign took up marijuana use, compared to 8 percent who had seen or participated in it. Slater believes this is due to the honest methods of the program and the focus on teens making their own decisions. "The 'Above the Influence' campaign appears to be successful because it taps into the desire by teenagers to be independent and self-sufficient,"[53] Slater said.

High school sophomore Allison Kufta thinks her peers will make smart decisions when they are presented with factual information similar to what Above the Influence provides. "[Some think that marijuana] isn't that dangerous because it doesn't have the same repercussions that alcohol does . . . or other more intensely affecting drugs like heroin, and they think that cannabis is like a lighter, not as dangerous thing," Kufta said. "I think if people were more aware of this, they would care more about their future and their awareness of this contemporary world issue and be smarter."[54]

As of 2014 the Above the Influence program was being run by the not-for-profit Partnership for Drug-Free Kids. This organization has continued the media campaign and various efforts to communicate with teens about marijuana and encourage them to make smart choices.

Parental Involvement

Even the programs that successfully discourage drug experimentation by teens can only go so far. Studies suggest that parent involvement is key. Parents can have a big effect on their kids' thinking about experimenting with marijuana. When the Partnership for Drug-Free Kids released its annual tracking study, it discussed what young people said stopped them from trying drugs. The two most common reasons young people chose not to use marijuana were getting into trouble with the law and disappointing their parents.

How parents should talk to their kids is debated. Experts suggest that they be open and honest about the dangers and risks of drug use and about the pressures that friends and classmates can exert. However, some professionals argue against parents talking about their own drug use, if they ex-

Most experts agree that parents are a key factor in keeping their children off drugs. Mothers and fathers openly discussing the dangers of drug use and the pressures to partake in drugs can help teens feel confident in choosing to refrain from using marijuana and other illegal substances.

perimented with drugs as a teen. This is because surveys show that children of parents who use marijuana are more likely to try it themselves.

According to a 2014 survey done for the Hazelden Betty Ford Foundation Center for Public Advocacy, 72 percent of young adults surveyed who reported using marijuana said their parents are current or past marijuana users. A 2013 University of Illinois at Urbana–Champaign survey also found that youth who knew about their parents' past drug use were less likely to view drug use as risky. The Illinois researchers surveyed 561 middle school students on talks they had had with their parents about drinking, smoking, and marijuana. The researchers discovered that youth were less likely to consider drugs dangerous if their parents had told them stories of their own drug use.

Already Addicted

In addition to programs and methods to prevent marijuana experimentation, there are programs for teens who have already experimented and become addicts or abusers. Both inpatient and outpatient treatment programs are available to help teens stop their addiction and break the cycle of use. Among youth receiving substance abuse treatment, marijuana accounts for the largest percentage of admissions. Adolescent admissions for treatment of marijuana-related problems increased from 63 percent of adolescent admissions in 2002 to 76 percent in 2012, according to a Substance Abuse and Mental Health Services Administration report.

Newport Academy is one example of a program that offers inpatient and outpatient treatment for teens at locations throughout the United States. The weekly outpatient program includes six hours of personal and family therapy, twelve hours of group therapy, and twelve hours of activities that might include yoga, martial arts, and art therapy. The teen remains at home and can attend his or her own school while getting treatment.

An inpatient program involves a teen living full time at a residential facility and typically involves a stay of thirty to forty-five days. A normal day involves group therapy, individual therapy, family therapy, schoolwork, 12-step meetings (similar to those conducted by Alcoholics Anonymous) and more. The goal is to help teens learn the underlying reasons for why they chose to use drugs, help them find other ways to deal with those issues, and establish communication between them and their parents. It took treatment for Rhianne to understand that, at age seventeen, she had a problem. "After a while, I realized that I was missing out on things other kids my age were doing, like going to the prom and playing sports, because I was stoned all the time. I was addicted to smoking pot,"[55] she explained when describing her progress at a treatment center.

> "After a while, I realized that I was missing out on things other kids my age were doing, like going to the prom and playing sports, because I was stoned all the time."[55]
>
> —Rhianne, a seventeen-year-old who underwent treatment for marijuana addiction.

Successful Program

An example of a highly successful treatment program is the Phoenix House Academy program offered by Phoenix House, a nonprofit treatment organization. The academy offers nine programs throughout the United States in which school and rehabilitation are combined. While teens live at the academies, they continue their schoolwork and receive intensive group and individual counseling to help them break their habits and understand how to deal with their addiction. In 2005 the US Department of Justice designated the Phoenix House Academy as a model program due to its success.

The program is not easy for teens who attend it, but many attest to its success. Alex started using marijuana at thirteen, and his use increased as he also got involved in other drugs. By the time he was seventeen, his entire life centered on drugs. He confessed this to his family, and they encouraged him to go to a Phoenix House Academy. Alex did not want to, but eventually said he would try it. "The first few days I was kind of miserable. I told myself, It's going to get worse before it gets better. Just stick it out to the end. I'm glad I did," said Alex. "Phoenix House showed me the Narcotics Anonymous program. They taught me how to deal with certain triggers that make me want to use, how to deal with anger and other emotions. It made me unhappy— but it showed me how to deal with being unhappy."[56] After he left the Phoenix House Academy, Alex was able to graduate from high school, and he began attending college.

After a teen leaves a treatment program, the success of the program depends on how involved parents are with the teen, if the teen continues with aftercare programs, and if the teen continues to use the tools he or she obtained through the program. To ensure his success, Alex continued to go to Narcotics Anonymous meetings, communicated with his family, and applied what he learned from his stay at the Phoenix House Academy.

Barriers to Treatment

Although treatment for teen marijuana addiction can be successful, it can also be difficult to attain. According to an analysis by Closing the Addiction Treatment Gap, 1 million teens need drug treatment, but only one in ten actually end up getting any type of treatment. One reason is the lack of state and federal funding for youth treatment programs. Another issue is that health insurance benefits for drug treatment are shrinking, making treatment difficult for families to afford. The result of these issues is that although many teens are in need of treatment, they are not always able to get it. "There is no other disorder or disease that is as undertreated in adolescents as substance use disorders," said Samuel Ball, president and chief executive officer of CASAColumbia, an organization that researches addiction and treatments.

Quoted in National Council on Alcoholism and Drug Dependence, "Treatment for Teens with Substance Use Disorders Lacking." https://ncadd.org.

The Future

Ultimately, the best way to avoid addiction to marijuana is for teens to delay experimentation. That is the goal of the drug education programs and other methods, so that teens do not need the addiction programs. With marijuana more prevalent and available, experts believe the most effective way to discourage use is to focus on the facts and give teens choices. Time will tell if these programs are able to successfully influence teens' decisions.

Source Notes

Introduction: A Teen Trend

1. Quoted in Aly Weisman, "US Censors Miley Cyrus Smoking Pot While Accepting MTV Europe Award," Business Insider, November 11, 2013. www.businessinsider.com.

2. Quoted in Christina Garibaldi, "Miley Cyrus Knew Fans Would 'Love' If She Smoked Weed on EMA Stage," MTV News, November 14, 2013. www.mtv.com.

3. Quoted in Lisa Freedman, "Is Smoking Weed NBD?," Seventeen, March 11, 2014. www.seventeen.com.

4. Quoted in Freedman, "Is Smoking Weed NBD?"

5. Quoted in Arijan Alagic, "Peer Pressure, Marijuana Become High Risk for Teenagers," Spectator (student newspaper of West High School, Waterloo, Iowa), April 10, 2014. www.waterloo.k12.ia.us/schoolsites/thespectator/peer-pressure-marijuana-become-high-risk-for-teenagers.

6. Quoted in Tara Parker-Pope, "Legal Marijuana for Parents, but Not Their Kids," New York Times, August 18, 2014. www.nyt.com.

Chapter One: Teen Usage

7. Quoted in Foundation for a Drug Free World, "Real People, Real Stories," 2014. www.drugfreeworld.org.

8. Quoted in National Institute on Drug Abuse, "Sixty Percent of 12th Graders Do Not View Regular Marijuana Use as Harmful," December 18, 2013. www.drugabuse.gov.

9. Quoted in ThreeSixty Journalism, "When the Smoke Clears: What Are Teen Attitudes About Marijuana Use?," March 8, 2013. www.threesixtyjournalism.org.

10. Quoted in Caleb Hellerman, "Is Super Weed, Super Bad?," CNN, August 9, 2013. www.cnn.com.

11. Quoted in Sue Swanson, "Pot in Your Pantry? Marijuana Use in Toddlers and Teens," *Huffington Post*, October 20, 2014. www.huffingtonpost.com.

12. Quoted in Jaimie E. Goldstein, "Students Find Way to Secretly Smoke Marijuana in Class," CBS Denver, February 5, 2014. http://denver.cbslocal.com.

13. Quoted in Sharon Hernandez, "Elkhart Teen Shares Story of Frightening Experience Smoking Synthetic Marijuana," *Elkhart (IN) Truth*, June 21, 2014. www.elkharttruth.com.

14. Quoted in Steve Elliott, "Synthetic Marijuana Is Now Officially Illegal," Toke of the Town, March 1, 2011. www.toke ofthetown.com.

15. Quoted in Donna Gordon Blankenship, "Washington High School Students More Likely to Smoke Pot than Cigarettes: Survey," *Huffington Post*, March 14, 2013. www .huffingtonpost.com.

16. Quoted in Aylin Zafir, "Study: More Teens Smoking Pot than Cigarettes," *Time*, June 11, 2012. http://newsfeed.time.com.

17. Quoted in Parker-Pope, "Legal Marijuana for Parents, but Not Their Kids."

18. Quoted in Holly Eagleson, "High Times," *Seventeen*, 2012. www.seventeen.com.

19. Clay Zeigler, "Keeping Busy with Activities Can Help a Teen Avoid Drug Use," New Beginnings, March 5, 2012. www .newbeginningsshc.com.

Chapter Two: Major Influences

20. Quoted in Pat Reavy, "As Marijuana Laws Change, More Teens Think Drugs Are Safe," *Salt Lake City (UT) Deseret News*, February 8, 2014. www.deseretnews.com.

21. Quoted in Jeff Mapes, "Legalized Marijuana: Effect on Teens Looms Large in Oregon Campaign," *Portland (OR) Oregonian*, August 22, 2014. www.oregonlive.com.

22. Quoted in Reavy, "As Marijuana Laws Change, More Teens Think Drugs Are Safe."

23. Quoted in Jenn Karlman, "FOX 5 Proves Medical Marijuana Card 'Easy' to Get," Fox 5, April 25, 2013. http://fox5san diego.com.

24. Quoted in Jennifer Wing, "Little Known Medical Marijuana Loophole Allows Teens to Get Lots of Pot," KPLU, June 30, 2014. www.kplu.org.

25. Quoted in Eric Ditzian, "Seth Rogen: 'I Smoke a Lot of Weed When I Write,'" MTV News, September 30, 2011. www.mtv .com.

26. Quoted in PopCrunch, "Fans 'Disappointed' After One Direction Stars Zayn and Louis Are Caught Smoking Marijuana," May 28, 2014. www.popcrunch.com.

27. Quoted in ThreeSixty Journalism, "When the Smoke Clears."

28. Quoted in Maggie Roache, Nazareth Academy, and Brianna Yang, "Smoking Weed Could Cost Teens," *Huffington Post*, October 29, 2014. www.huffingtonpost.com.

29. Quoted in Ryan Jaslow, "Survey: 'Digital Peer Pressure' Fueling Drug, Alcohol Use in High School Students," CBS News, August 22, 2012. www.cbsnews.com.

30. Quoted in Joel Eisenbaum, "Teens Finding, Obtaining Drugs Through Instagram," KPRC, August 6, 2013. www .click2houston.com.

31. Quoted in Eagleson, "High Times."

32. Quoted in Anthony Rivas, "Teens Are Using Marijuana to Cope with Their Problems, but They Could End Up Worsening Them," Medical Daily, September 15, 2014. www .medicaldaily.com.

33. Quoted in Paul Meyer, "Three Teenagers Explain Why They Turned to Marijuana to Help Their Medical Conditions," AlterNet, October 26, 2012. www.alternet.org.

34. Quoted in Catey Hill, "Doctors Recommend Medical Marijuana for Minors with ADHD in California," *New York Daily News*, November 25, 2009. www.nydailynews.com.

Chapter Three: The Consequences of Marijuana Use

35. Quoted in David Remnick, "Going the Distance," *New Yorker*, January 27, 2014. www.newyorker.com.

36. Quoted in Sharon Jayson, "Pot Studies Suggest Regular Use Is Bad for Teen Brains," *USA Today*, August 9, 2014. www.usatoday.com.

37. Quoted in National Institute on Drug Abuse, "NIDA Notes: Researchers Speak—Dr. Madeline Meier on Marijuana and IQ," August 2013. www.drugabuse.gov.

38. Quoted in Dennis Thompson, "Brain Scan Study Suggests Pothead Stereotype May Be Real," HealthDay, December 16, 2013. http://consumer.healthday.com.

39. Quoted in Wendy Swanson, "Marijuana Mixer, Teen Use, Child Ingestion," Seattle Children's Hospital, October 15, 2014. http://seattlemamadoc.seattlechildrens.org.

40. Quoted in Andrea Dukakis, "Denver Emergency Room Doctor Seeing More Patients for Marijuana Edibles," Colorado Public Radio, April 29, 2014. www.cpr.org.

41. Quoted in Christina Zdanowicz, "Teen Makes Dramatic Recovery After Smoking Synthetic Marijuana," CNN, September 11, 2013. www.cnn.com.

42. Quoted in Michael Winerip, "High Season: Teens and Marijuana Use," *Family Circle*, 2014. www.familycircle.com.

43. Quoted in Winerip, "High Season."

44. Quoted in Ludovica Iaccino, "Teens Who Smoke Cannabis Daily 'Seven Times More Likely to Commit Suicide,'" *International Business Times*, September 11, 2014. www.ibtimes.co.uk.

45. Quoted in Elaina Clarke, "Passion for Poker 'Saved My Life,' Greg Merson Says," *Baltimore (MD) Sun*, October 28, 2012. http://articles.baltimoresun.com.

46. Quoted in Lee Myers, "Teen Who Helped Run Ohio Drug Ring Will Serve Time," *USA Today*, October 22, 2012. www.usatoday.com.

Chapter Four: Reducing Teen Usage

47. Emily Knowlton, "An Opinion from a Teenager Above the Influence," *Teen Ink*. www.teenink.com.

48. Quoted in Erika Alexander, "Famous Fried Eggs," CNN, December 6, 2000. www.cnn.com.

49. Quoted in German Lopez, "Why Anti-Drug Campaigns like DARE Fail," Vox, September 1, 2014. www.vox.com.

50. Quoted in Sasha Foo, "Report Shows Weed Use Among Teens Higher than Ever," KUSI News, April 16, 2014. www.kusi.com.

51. Don't Be a Lab Rat, "What Does Weed Do to the Teenage Brain?" http://dontbealabrat.com.

52. Quoted in Maanvi Singh, "Colorado Tries Hard to Convince Teens That Pot Is Bad for You," NPR, September 9, 2014. www.npr.org.

53. Quoted in Ohio State University, "National Anti-drug Campaign Succeeds in Lowering Marijuana Use, Study Suggests," 2011. http://researchnews.osu.edu.

54. Quoted in Maggie Roache, "Smoking Weed Could Cost Teens," *Mash*, October 16, 2014. http://themash.com.

55. Quoted in Suzanna Williams, "You Can Get Addicted to Pot," Scholastic, 2014. www.scholastic.com.

56. Alex, "True Story: Alex," Phoenix House, August 28, 2014. www.phoenixhouse.org.

American Academy of Adolescent and Child Psychiatry

3615 Wisconsin Ave. NW
Washington, DC 20016-3007
phone: (202) 966-7300
website: www.aacap.org

This organization provides information about how drugs and alcohol affect teens and children. It discusses the warning signs of use and suggests ways to deal with youth use.

Drug Policy Alliance

925 Fifteenth St. NW, 2nd Floor
Washington, DC 20005
phone: (202) 683-2030
website: www.drugpolicy.org

This organization is dedicated to promoting drug law reform. It works toward states making their own choices regarding marijuana without federal oversight and provides information on legalization status throughout the United States.

Marijuana Policy Project

PO Box 77492
Capitol Hill
Washington, DC 20013
phone: (202) 462-5747
e-mail: info@mpp.org
website: www.mpp.org

This organization's goal is to pass federal medical marijuana legislation, as well as to replace marijuana prohibition with what it considers a system of sensible regulation and control. The organization provides information about its work throughout the United States regarding marijuana laws.

Monitoring the Future

Regents of the University of Michigan
Ann Arbor, MI 48109
website: www.monitoringthefuture.org

This organization conducts and publishes surveys regarding health in the United States. It provides annual national trends in smoking, drinking, and illicit drug use among American secondary school students.

National Institute on Drug Abuse

6001 Executive Blvd.
Room 5213, MSC 9561
Bethesda, MD 20892-9561
phone: (301) 443-1124
website: www.drugabuse.gov

This organization is a government agency leading the United States in its fight against drug abuse. It provides the latest study results of the effects of drug use and information on programs both to prevent drug abuse and help those already addicted.

National Survey on Drug Use and Health

website: https://nsduhweb.rti.org

The National Survey on Drug Use and Health provides national and state-level data on the use of tobacco, alcohol, illicit drugs (including nonmedical use of prescription drugs), and mental health in the United States. It is sponsored by the Substance Abuse and Mental Health Services Administration.

Partnership for Drug-Free Kids

352 Park Ave. S., 9th Floor
New York, NY 10010
e-mail: communications@drugfree.org
website: www.drugfree.org

This organization is dedicated to stopping teen drug use and provides information and statistics about youth drug use and its dangers. It also gives information about its campaigns against drug use.

Smart Colorado

PO Box 803
Englewood, CO 80151
e-mail: info@smartcolorado.org
website: www.smartcolorado.org

Smart Colorado's mission is to protect the health and safety of Colorado youth as marijuana becomes more available in the state. This organization works to implement laws that it believes will protect youth from marijuana. It also provides information on Colorado's current marijuana laws and their impacts on youth.

Books

Lydia Bjornlund, *Marijuana*. San Diego: ReferencePoint, 2011.

Steve Fox, Paul Armentano, and Mason Tvert, *Marijuana Is Safer: So Why Are We Driving People to Drink?* White River Junction, VT: Chelsea Green, 2013.

Frederick Gross, *The Truth About Marijuana*. New York: Rosen, 2011.

Marin Lee, *Smoke Signals: A Social History of Marijuana— Medical, Recreational and Scientific*. New York: Scribner, 2012.

Mickey Martin, *Medical Marijuana 101*. Oakland, CA: Quick American, 2011.

Internet Sources

Center for Brain Health, "Study Shows Marijuana's Long-Term Effects on the Brain," November 10, 2014. www.brainhealth .utdallas.edu/blog_page/study-shows-marijuanas-long-term -effects-on-the-brain.

Bernie DeGroat, "Peer Influence: Facebook, Twitter, Alcohol and Drugs," University of Michigan, 2014. www.ns.umich.edu /new/releases/20877-peer-influence-facebook-twitter-alcohol -and-drugs.

Jim Dryden, "Youth Regularly Receive Pro-marijuana Tweets," Washington University in St. Louis, June 27, 2014. http://news .wustl.edu/news/Pages/27077.aspx.

Steve Nelson, "Pot Legalization: Gateway to What?," *U.S. News & World Report*, November 12, 2014. www.usnews.com /news/articles/2014/11/12/pot-legalization-gateway-to-what.

Alexandra Pannoni, "3 Ways High Schools Are Combating Marijuana Use," *U.S. News & World Report*, September 15, 2014. www.usnews.com/education/blogs/high-school-notes /2014/09/15/3-ways-high-schools-are-combating-marijuana -use.

WebMD, "How Does Marijuana Affect You?," www.webmd .com/mental-health/addiction/marijuana-use-and-its-effects.

Saundra Young, "Frequent Teen Marijuana Use Linked to Is- sues Later in Life," CNN, September 10, 2014. www.cnn.com /2014/09/09/health/teen-marijuana-use.

Websites

Above the Influence (www.abovetheinfluence.com). This website provides the latest media programs that the organiza- tion is using to discourage teen drug and alcohol use.

Don't Be a Lab Rat (http://dontbealabrat.com). This website provides information about the risks of marijuana for youth, as well as the latest in its program against teen drug use.

K2 Zombie DC (http://k2zombiedc.com). This website pro- vides information about the dangers of synthetic marijuana, along with its campaign against teen use.

Index

stress and usage, 8–9, 32–34, **33**
Substance Abuse and Mental Health Services Administration, 61
suicidal thoughts, 46–47
Sukle, Mike, 57
Synthetic Drug Abuse Prevention Act (2012), 19
synthetic marijuana, **43**
    average age of user of, 57
    composition of, 18, 42–43
    effects of, 18, 43, 44
    legality of, 18–19
    overdoses, 43–44
    overview of, 18

Teerlink, Doug, 25
tetrahydrocannabinol (THC), 12–13, 14, 36
Thamba, Levy, 9
This Is Your Brain on Drugs campaign, 53–54
Timberlake, Justin, 29
tobacco use, decrease in, 20
treatment programs, 61–63
12-step programs, 62, 63

usage
    decrease in after legalization for adults, 27
    increase in
        after legalization for adults, 25, 26–27
        in high school (1991 to 2013), 8
        by high school grade (2012 to 2013), 12

by twelfth graders (2008 to 2013), 20
methods of, 14–17, **17**
by parents and, 37, 61
of synthetic marijuana, 19
See also medicinal usage; recreational usage
US Department of Health and Human Services, 20

vapor pens, 16–17, **17**
vasculitis, 44
Volkow, Nora D., 11–12, 21

Walking Dead, The (television program), 57
Washington State
    medical marijuana cards, 29
    perception of risk decreased after legalization, 25–26
    state-approved edibles, 16
    tobacco and alcohol compared to marijuana use, 20
Washington, DC, 24–25, 57
water pipes, 15
Weatherly, Paul, 29
Williams, Greg, 46
withdrawal symptoms, 46

Youth Risk Behavior Surveillance System (2013), 8

Zane, Richard, 42
Zeigler, Clay, 23
Zhang, Alex, 26
Zidow, Christina, 27
zombies campaign, 57–58

Picture Credits

Leanne Currie-McGhee resides in Norfolk, Virginia, with her husband and two children, Grace and Hope. She has written more than twenty educational books.

1-800-913-3750

711-7921-381

011 251 911 23-81-25 - Samuel

22-36-41 - Hatu